GARDENS GROW THROUGH THE HEART

Gardens Grow Through The Heart

PRESLY N PHILLIPS

GARDENS GROW THROUGH THE HEART

BY: PRESLY PHILLIPS

DEDICATED TO THOSE WHO
ARE GOING THROUGH
THEIR HEALING PROCESS

Gardens Grow Through the Heart

Vines grew out of my heart,
until flowers burst through my skin.
It has stretched me so far,
that my body has worn thin.

My tears through my pain,
has created rain for years.
It has watered my garden,
until my whole soul became a forest.

I have been killed many times,
but I grew back with more thorns.
My soul is a forest of roses and thorns.
If you dare to pass now, you will be torn.

Beware of the woman with vines in her veins,
because deadly flowers can cause worlds of pain.

The Heart's Restart

I've ripped my heart out of my chest,
to start over once again.
I set fire to my brain,
to rid myself of all the pain.

Cleansed by the moonlight,
in the middle of my darkness.
Reborn through the sun's fire,
after years of crippling sadness.

I sucked the poison out of my veins,
to give my lungs a chance.
Stopped drinking the damage,
to make my liver dance.

I've turned myself inside out,
to examine the years of damage I've done.
I will mend my body till its death,
and start the rebirth that has already begun.

Wear My Flowers Like a Crown

I cover my eyes with flowers.
Dance in my brain for hours.
Write about poems and pain.
Cry so much, the bugs think it's rain.

Sensitive minds run emotions high.
My brain constantly thinks the end is nigh.
There are things about life I'll never understand.
It makes me want to hold my heart in my hand.

Dreaming creates beautiful lives.
Reality seems to create horrid lies.
Perhaps I can blend the dream and what is real.
Stop hiding from all that I feel.

I will pluck the flowers from my eyes,
and wear them as a crown.
I will climb up the vines,
every time I fall down.

The Sad Story of the Beauty Named Eve

Wandering around the woods,
Eve cried for help.
Her eyes were covered in vines,
no one could hear her yelp.

She reached for an apple,
it was filled with poison and dread.
Eating the apple infected her head.
Dropping it to stumble upon the tree.

Animals surrounded a sleeping beauty,
crying over the death of Eve.
They say her tears were petals,
and her heart became a tree.

The story of a beauty turned into the embodiment of sin.
No one noticed how she was horridly thin.
Nature was hungry and she tried to feed.
All to die anyways for societies blameful need.

Comfortable Lives

I lay on the ground like a corpse,
waiting to be swept up and buried underground.
Somehow the wood felt soft,
and the sun felt like a cold breeze.

The birds were singing a sad melody,
about the girl who felt ready to die in the woods.
Buried by leaves and carried off by trees.
Her ashes flowing through the breeze.

If I wake up after this sickness,
will I ever be the same?
Could I possibly just be a girl,
who was found in the woods without a name?

Sometimes such a melancholy feeling can feel like beauty.
Where sickness makes the body tingle with comfort.
I no longer know if I am comfortable with sadness or happiness.
Perhaps I will learn how to be equally comfortable in both.

Patched With Flowers

I've fallen from the sky,
and landed on my back.
Rolled through the grass,
until I got back on track.

I picked myself up and bandaged my cuts with flowers.
Went looking for some water to quench a dreadful thirst.
It feels as if I've walked this deserted trail for hours.
Apart of me has been missing for years.

Like my soul remained in the sky.
I may still be broken, suffering to the bone.
However, I am finally whole.
I've fallen many times, but I continue to get back up.

Healed by nature over and over again.

Where the Wildflowers Grow

My mouth can be silent,
as the flowers grow from it rather violent.
It is from my heart where bushels grow,
until eventually nature begins to show.

My veins are vines, and my body is a tree.
That is why in nature is when I feel free.
I've been saved from fallen leaves.
My soul floats to the sky when I breathe.

Awakened by the sun,
comforted by the moon.
No longer afraid of life beginning soon.
My mind is rid of impending doom.

My dreams have become stars that patiently shine.
My shadows have left their sorrow behind.
I walk like a wildflower among a garden of roses.
All living significant lives that nature has chosen.

Soft

You don't need to be soft-headed or hard hearted.
You don't need to be gentle,
when someone is playing a game.

You don't need to smile,
when you feel like crying.
You don't need to pretend that you love living,
when you wish to be dying.

You don't need to be okay.
You don't need to be soft in the eyes of others.
But darling,
just be soft on yourself.

Flowers fall but never falter.
Vines grow underneath tons of soil.
Trees form after dying twenty times.
Rising above ground after years of rain.

You have fallen but never faltered.
You've grown underneath tons of troubles.
Your soul forms after dying twenty times.
You will rise above years of pain.

Surgery to Heal

I want to love myself to death.
Kill my aching brain with every breath.
Tear out my heart to begin the mend.
Cut out my brain to bend.

A metaphorical doctor starts surgery.
Without the numbing of my body.
Feeling all the pains of mending bones.
Searching for the wounds that have shown.

I've sewn my heart shut,
and returned it to my chest.
Patched up my brain with tape,
shoved it back into my skull.

Breathing slowly with my new organs.
Broken inside but mended just the same.
Healing is a long journey for the insane.
However, I am ready to live again.

Bushels of Berries Bleed

I dream of bushels of berries waking up.
Yawning and stretching their wings.
Waiting for the tree's freedom rings.
Then they fly high in the sky.

As I sleep, stories are told.
Tales of fairies and mermaids unfold.
How the queen of the trees sings at night.
While the moon becomes her night light.

I dream that a rose's death has beauty.
Resting its petals on the ground.
I will tie it around my head, wear it as a crown.
Roses and berries make a reign.

As I stand under the sun, the berries will bleed.
It'll look like my dead roses are crying blood.
A woman of nature is beautifully grotesque.
This is my untold dream, I must confess.

A Witch's Connection

Plants grow from her head,
she sleeps on a flower bed.
Picks herbs to leave her demons at bay.
Drinks tea to start the day.

She charges her crystals in the moonlight.
Look to the moon for guidance at night.
A black cat watches nature from the window.
As the trees wither into willow.

The water flows, charging her heart.
The universe is trying not to fall apart.
Being one with nature can settle the brain.
To lose that connection makes a witch insane.

Power comes from self and Earth alike.
Connection comes from the cosmic light.
A witch has vines growing from her feet.
Her relationship with nature is mysteriously steep.

A Bittersweet Goodbye

I carried my broken self through the forest inside my heart.
She was covered in scrapes and had tears frozen on her cheeks.
Everything she felt, she felt incredibly deep.
Her mind bled so much it killed her.

I laid her on the dirt ground and began to bury her.
Covering her body with the Earth's soil.
Decorating her grave with as many flowers as I could.
Shedding tears that added to hers on her cheek.

Her face looked like a sky full of stars,
frozen tears and years of tortured souls.
Before I buried her face, I kissed her forehead.
Wished her a better life in the afterlife.

From this form of self-care, I was risen.
Every bit of the goodbye hurt like a thousand swords.
At last, my broken heart can rest,
and maybe my own mind will finally rest.

Grotesque Restart

Pulled the knife out of my chest.
Ripped my heart from my breast.
Buried it in the dirt.
Walked away heartless until it hurt.

My heart grew into a tree.
Watered in the rain like a seed.
The leaves kept screaming for me.
Inside my chest is where it wanted to be.

Without my heart, my soul went cold.
My brain turned to snow.
There were no emotions to show.
I had to return my heart before I froze.

I ran to the tree in the rain,
dug through the mud until my arms felt pain.
Bleeding so much the blood pooled.
Death made me look like a fool.

Unburied my mended heart,
cut open my chest,
shoved my heart back above my breast.
I have been reborn grotesquely but can begin to restart.

DAISES REVENGE

Daises get stepped on.
Day after day.
They wait for the water,
in the month of May.

After the rain comes a poisonous haze.
As souls drop to the ground,
the daises chant, and dance.
All the times they were kicked to the ground,
their pollen got stronger.

It is the daises revenge
to make evil no longer.

The Skeleton at a Desk

A writer writes till their bones break.
Till they are a skeleton at a desk,
surrounded with canvases of paint,
and blood stains on their sleeves.

They write pain so much they bleed ink.
Their heart falls out of their chest,
and is used as their stamp.
To send their story to anyone who listens.

The record player keeps skipping,
as the writer scratches their brain.
They cannot fix it,
because they need to write their pain.

A writer is glued to a paper.
Their pen is a part of their bones.
Disintegrating into the desk,
until every grotesque bone is shown.

The Crying Statue

Once upon a time there was a beautiful statue.
Carved in such unnatural beauty.
This artwork was worshiped by many.
None knew if she was true.

A lady with gold trimmed mold.
A heart in her hands started to unfold.
There are legends the people are told.
About a woman who is decades old.

The artist never told a soul who she was.
Loved to keep the woman as a mystery.
A figure that would never be in history.
Just a woman standing in a meadow.

So many people studied this beauty.
The statue followed through her duty.
To stand lonely among the flowers through the years.
If you look closely, you can see her sad tears.

Tree of Eternity

There is a tree growing in my rib cage,
waiting for the day it may burst free.
My heart is its life source,
for it is eternally grateful.

Millions of seeds create life inside my body.
Blooming wildly and free.
Some days it hurts and some days it is calming.
Yet all of it is equally me.

My mouth has no reason to speak,
because my mind is doing all the talking.
It tells the story of the seasons inside me.
How the tree dances with my heart's beat.

Each of us are an embodiment of nature.
All little trees in a giant forest.
One day our bodies will die but the tree will live,
and for that, our souls will be eternal.

Little Songbird

The little songbird flapped her wings desperately,
surviving on what seems to be a tiny heartbeat.
Women have more lives beneath their breasts,
that causes their hearts to beat out of their chest.

But the little songbird had a heart so small,
it pumped with deep yet little love.
Unable to sing love songs, only sad melodies.
For it was cursed to have its notes ripped out with every love tale.

It flew with melancholy,
finding little loves through the flowers it sat upon.
Dreading the winter for its loves will parish,
leaving the little songbird utterly alone.

With frozen feathers and a heart so small,
it sang its sad tunes.
Forever a lullaby for the lonely woods.

Seasonal Depression

In the winter, we wait to thaw.
Our brains itch and our heart freezes.
As we hibernate in the warmth,
like a sleeping bear who hates the cold.

We try our best to not let our tears fall,
in fear that it will freeze to our cheeks.
Leaving our hearts truly on our sleeves,
viewable to every love thief.

It is among the snow that our hearts are bare.
We grow targets on our heads,
to secret predators looking for vulnerability.
In search of a cold and lonely soul.

We must focus on wonders winter has,
to not dwindle and go mad.
Keep warmth in our bodies so our hearts do not freeze.
Survive until there is no longer a chilling breeze.

A Field of Poppies

She collapsed from exhaustion,
rose petals flying through the air.
Falling always but never seeming to land.
It only seems that rest is after death.

With dark circled eyes,
and low soft energy.
She remains in bed for eternity,
yet never seeming to get enough sleep.

The sleeping beauty that fell from the sky,
is simply waiting for her demise.
Falling and falling, sinking to the ground.
Yet it never seems to make a single sound.

A somnolent fallen angel,
who seems to have demons in her brain.
Breathes in the smell of flowers,
falling under the field of poppies spell.

We need to breathe.

Rest is not mindless,
it is for the mind to feed.
To process thoughts and needs.
Productivity is seen in a search within.

To stand still is difficult,
we get restless when we feel incompetent.
It causes our stomachs to stir,
and our nerves become shot.

We tear off so much of our bodies,
to feel like we have made something of ourselves.
We cry many rivers to feel,
to prove to the world that we are alive.

We've become exhausted and stripped of our might.
Too busy pushing through instead of healing.
They say laziness is death,
when really, we need the rest.

So, we may breathe.

Contently Drifting

I am contently drifting,
floating down a river filled with my own tears.
Holding a bouquet of dead flowers,
of failed lovers throughout the years.

As I slowly let the flowers go,
they move on to different streams.
I let my arms out in freedom,
drifting lonely on the water.

There are things my heart cannot bear to feel.
My melancholy gets inconsolably real.
However, I am more comfortable there.
Rather be in a lonely river than the entire sea.

I am drowning in contentedness.
My body is filled with stillness and silence.
I may be floating down the river alone,
but I am comforted by the water below.

Bleeding Hearts Nurture Trees

Elusive imagery falls from my head,
like a light leaking from my heart,
that appears blood red.
Is it love or is it death?

Perhaps my heart is decaying,
or perhaps it is rapidly beating.
Stitched together with pins and needles,
causing my love to be too sharp to share.

Romantic love is something my heart cannot bear.
Yet it bleeds, yet it loves.
Forever flowing out to the abyss,
becoming water for the trees.

I may never fall in love.
However, nature will always feel my love.
Until eventually I fall into the dirt,
becoming the very thing I could only love.

The Rose's Story

I always look at roses so bittersweet.
How beautiful they are, yet they were plucked from their homes.
Their dying bodies become decorations,
for lovers yet they remain alone.

Silently wondering, haven't I given enough of my petals?
Why must lovers treat us with such disregard?
Shouldn't they show us love by planting us, letting us grow?
But no... we are just for show.

They ask to just let us be drowned,
float in water at least, yet they die of thirst.
Without their home to belong,
they remain in lovers' homes, utterly alone.

Observing

Oh, how boringly still I can be.
Content in the woods or indoors.
A comfort in slight loneliness.
Living in a black and white world, with an appreciation for color.

How beautiful this world can be when you simply observe.
Like looking at a painting in a museum.
Making any dull heart fill up with red.
Like how a melody sticks in your busy head.

However, dull I may seem,
my mind is filled with colors.
Acrylics painted over the brain,
so, I may see the world as beauty.

Observing a duality of emotions.
Sorrow, dread, happiness, a bittersweet combo.
Wishing upon a star to let me observe always.
Both beauty and melancholy are things I must see.

Under My Skin

There are roses growing underneath my skin.
Vines growing up my spine,
flowers blooming around my skull.
A decorated skeleton underneath me.

Nature saved me, as it has grown within me.
A garden spreading around the soul.
A whole universe is inside me.
The type of energy that drives the seasons.

Each soul is a part of Earth,
the very makeup of it is inside us.
Once I learned this, I realized I was whole all along.
There was nothing missing, I just was told wrong.

I am nature, one day the vines will puncture through my skin.
I'll replenish the Earth in the dirt when my life ends.
It is then I will live once again,
until then, I will continue to bloom every day.

The Heart in The Tree

Who put her heart in the willow tree?
And why is it still beating rapidly?
The movement is causing the leaves to fall,
creating a circle around the trunk.

If you look closely, it looks as if the trees are breathing,
yet it is just her heart still beating.
Who buried her heart where this tree grew?
Perhaps she put it there herself for safe keeping.

So many unanswered questions.
Like how is it still bleeding?
How is she still breathing?
Can we possibly live without our hearts?

Perhaps it is a woman who turned into a tree,
like how people replenish the Earth's soil when they die.
She replenished the willow tree in fear of its death.
So, she switched her grave-site before her last breath.

Valentine's Day

Around me, hearts intertwine their vines.
Blending the beats of their life.
Dancing to the sound of no melody.
Like their mind is playing the same tune.

Yet my heart is alone in the woods.
With vines that have been chopped,
and are slowly growing back.
Blood beating to my own tune.

Everyone is falling in love,
and I am dancing on my own.
Listening to the senses of nature,
falling through the trees.

As I fall,
I pass my lovers in each vine.
I shall continue to drop without one to call mine.
Yet, I still left loneliness behind.

Molded to Heal

I have created and molded myself out of the mud,
from the dirt that has been cleansed by the rain.
Growing my roots into the center of the Earth,
solidifying in the middle of the woods.

Becoming a statue in the middle of the forest.
Allowing vines to grow on my limbs,
like a garden sculpture alone in the trees.
Waiting to thaw when my heart is ready.

The mold is protecting my bleeding heart,
like a band aid made from nature.
Hibernating inside the sculpture,
until my heart finally healed.

One day my mold will melt off,
and my heart will heal and thaw.
My feet will break off from my roots,
and I will rise again.

There are words carved into my rib cage,
telling tales and legends of humanity.
Molded to survive eternity,
remain on my bones as I rot.

That way a grave robber will find no gold,
but the words on my bones.
Perhaps they will tell the world the history of my dreams,
or perhaps they will bury my rib cage back.

For the next poor soul that'll happen upon the words of a skeleton.

Mother Nature's Voice

Nature has a voice for those who listen.
Whispering stories in their ears,
as the trees make their eyes glisten.
Filling what has been missing for eternity.

The woods become a home for lost souls.
A call that leads the wanderers.
Like the vines under the soil are constantly whispering,
luring the hearts that grow leaves.

Whenever they sleep the roots of the Earth connect again.
Charging the soul as the vessel sleeps.
Their body like a beautiful tree trunk,
that holds a remarkable heart.

Even in utter silence,
nature will always call soul's home.
Listen to your body when it needs to be recharged,
because as you fall nature will always catch you.

Bloom and Decay

Roses sprout from her chest in the spring,
like her body is their decomposing soil.
Constantly changing with her drifting mortality.
Blooming and decaying throughout the seasons.

When you look closely you can see art breathe.
She is the living embodiment of nature.
Both brilliance and grotesque.
Like nature, she is both nurturing and cruel.

Savagely growing thorns to protect her skin.
Wrapping her rib cage in vines,
so that if her body dies, her art will stay intact.
A beautiful fossil in the dirt.

A skeleton with roses sprouting from her rib cage,
as her skin becomes decomposed soil.
A changed beauty with immortality.
Both bloomed and decayed for her last season.

Swimming

I am finally a stranger to my grief.
No longer swimming in defeat,
finally brushing against the shore.
Gasping for fresh salty air.

Dragging myself through the sand on a lonely island.
Seclusion feels like freedom after years of tragedy.
The ability to be by oneself,
and not drown in grim thoughts.

I am no longer drowning.
I learned to swim against high tides.
Holding my breath long enough to come ashore.
To a new island that can be molded as mine.

I will build a new fort around my heart.
With windows to let the light in.
After I spit out the water from my lungs.
I will breathe steadily once again.

How strange the water lily is,
preferring to float in melancholy.
Alone in a pond without a pair.
Waiting to be whisked away by the fountain,
and drowned by the current.

Just so it can come alive again,
and continue that consistency.
How is it possible,
that this life is what makes the lily feel free.

The Relics of Mystery

Paintings are relics of warning,
of what is lurking in the shadows.
Secrets of life can be sinister,
everything about anything is slightly unknown.

Some thrive within the mystery,
while others cower from it.
Drinking and dumping used cigarettes in a glass box.
Sipping their coffee to stay alive.

They scribble nonsense on torn out pages.
Trying to make sense of such mysteries.
Poets are writing the thoughts that plague their brains.
All in search of one question; why are we here?

Positively negative of the morality of humans.
Yet infatuated with the duality of people.
The good and the bad, the mystery and the solved.
Leaving relics to tell others of a life forever unsolved.

Hibernation Underground

As I lay on the grass,
I slowly began to sink.
Further and further into the dirt,
like a grave was starting to surround me.

Above is nothing but the sky,
quickly disrupted by vines wrapping over my body.
Keeping me snug and covering me up.
Closing me within my sunken grave.

It is there, I hibernate for months.
Sleeping away the days and nights.
As thoughts swirl around,
and my insides work to keep me alive.

Preserved like a statue buried in the dirt.
Waiting for the sun to finally shine.
Once the flowers bloom, the vines release,
and I crawl myself out of the grave.

Within the Void

I find myself wishing I could close my eyes,
and open them in a galaxy full of stars.
A void state, where I feel as light as a feather,
and absolutely nothing weighs me down.

Where I feel like just a molecule in a big world,
with a predetermined Milky Way,
that'll lead me to peace.
All I must do is remain still.

To hibernate within the sky,
as tears drops fall from my eye.
Onto others it'll feel like rain,
but when they look up, they do not see pain.

Just stars lighting up a dark night,
and in that moment, everything feels right.
As I float among the planets I will smile with bliss,
because at last, there won't be a single thing I missed.

A Tree and A Soul

As the sun warms my skin,
it wears my dreary thoughts thin.
I can feel my soul flying,
like eagles do in the sky, soaring effortlessly.

The trees guide me, their limbs stretch out far.
Ready to catch me if I lose my balance.
As the grass creates a bed,
soft enough for when I do fall.

The birds sing a song,
when my ears hear nothing but silence.
The wind gives me breath,
when my own keeps catching.

The river cleans the dirt off my heart,
washes my brain so the wound isn't infected.
How nature creates so much nurture,
is beyond an explanation.

It is the closest connection to ourselves in living form.

Internal Rest

I wish for eternal slumber,
like a masterpiece shattered on the table.
A lily floating on the waves.
Blissful rest, to finally rejuvenate.

Like cream sitting on top of coffee,
flowers swaying in the wind.
To feel as if I am weightless,
no longer feeling the heaviness of gravity.

I want the relief of rest.
The softness after years in the storms.
To feel like the raindrops and not the thunder.
I finally feel like I can be still.

Wishing for time to stop with me,
so, I can feel the sun on my face.
Breathe in a gentle breath,
and breathe out with blissful ease.

Oceans Magic

Divinity is the song the oceans sing.
Washing away all the negativity.
Purifying my body with salt and fresh water.
Rejuvenating my very soil.

The mysteries that swim in the deep water,
will take your pain to the ocean floor.
No one may enter or else they will be crushed.
Therefore, your problems will be sincerely flushed.

How the sea calls for lost souls,
for their hearts need to be repaired.
Their minds need to be cleansed and charged.
I will plunge myself into the water filled with salt.

Inside I will see many worlds,
a connection to mystery upon this Earth.
My home is within the unknown.
I belong with the creatures of the sea, forever unseen.

Blooming

Violent vibrations can be heard from my chest,
as threads of my split heart reaches for the other.
Sewing up my messy bleeding heart.
The blood feeding my insides.

Replenished in a grotesque way,
molding and mending from years of pain.
Covered in stains and scratches,
yet whole just the same.

More than a body, but my mind is its essence.
A soul walking among the Earth.
We are creatures of the world,
as interesting and compelling as the next.

On the outside, I am a woman,
but on the inside, I am a burst of stars.
Sewn together with vines and thorns.
From my wounds, I have bloomed flowers.

The Forest in my Mind

I searched through the forest in my mind.
Found both wonders and nightmares.
The duality of the forest used to scare me,
but I've learned to love it in its darkness as well as its light.

The trees change throughout the seasons.
Hibernating in the cold, blood greater in the warmth.
It's softness and strength are equally beautiful.
I've found humility within my eerie forest.

Nature is gloriously unpredictable,
while keeping a ritual.
Telling me I do not need to be one thing,
and answer to no one but my mind's forest.

I had to be lost in the woods to be found.
Nature feeds my leafy mind.
As thoughts swirl like the wind,
becoming water for my thirsty heart.

Words of Melancholy

She was dreamy melancholy trapped in a bottle.
Filled with un-romantic passion.
A big heart that only bleeds for platonic love,
yet it fills rivers and oceans.

Her mind is a cloud,
raining thoughts of bittersweet stories.
Her voice is only seen on paper,
like her mouth has been tapped shut.

Quite a tragic little poet who dug herself out.
Digging herself out of the dirt.
Like artwork that survived fire,
despite losing pieces of herself in the ash.

Happiness is found through tragedy.
Only one can dream when they felt extreme melancholy.
Her heart is exquisite yet flawed.
It will always beat and bleed the words she cannot say.

Sleeping Beauty

Sleeping beauty asleep on the grass.
Let me lie with the vines in my shallow grave.
As the rain falls on my tingly face,
reminding me being buried is temporary.

As I breathe in, my heart eats dirt.
Planting seeds so my heart may burst.
I must grow from the bottom of the Earth,
blooming from my body to the sky.

To be asleep in nature,
is to find comfort in silence.
As if I swallowed dirt in my grave,
Yet in silence my brain feeds.

Thoughts are being fed by watered soil.
My heart is blooming out of my chest.
onlookers may see a grotesque death,
But it is my rebirth after my rest.

I Want to Un-Apologize

I want to be brutally unapologetic,
about how I want my life to be.
No longer hiding behind what society wants me to be.
An innocent vessel, a body with a heart.

I am more than a pre-determined life,
a list a woman must follow.
More than a body with a beating heart,
but the embodiment of nature.

We are taught that we must answer to someone,
ask for permission for simple things.
I don't have to answer to anyone but myself.
I will not ask permission to live my life as I wish.

My cruelty is in selfishness and my softness is in caring.
Brutally humble in living my life.
I will regrow my limbs every time I fail.
With the freedom to experience all life has to offer.

What I Consume

Toss your insults in my heart,
they will dissolve in the acidic rain.
Turn to liquid in my veins.
Cleansed by the blood before it gets to my brain.

My body has learned to protect me through the years.
Like how plants give oxygen to the living.
Despite the pain, my heart remains beating.
Growing a forest of vines in my insides.

Whisper your opinions in my ear,
my eardrums have been drowning them out for years.
My mind is made up and my heart agrees,
I'll plant my garden the way I want.

My watered heart will flourish,
with the nourishment my body chooses.
What feeds me may not feed you.
However, it is my life, and I'll choose what I consume.

The Woman in The Tree

If you put your ear to the tree,
you can hear a woman inside weep.
As the bark scratches your ear,
you can hear a heart faintly beat.

You wish you could dig a hole inside the tree,
create a door to break the woman free.
Yet she is stuck inside, not wishing to get out.
She cannot bear to see what has become of her nature.

Every dying soul and living thing chips away at her heart.
That is why it thumps faintly,
dying of heartbreak each day.
She fears the world has forgotten her.

Finding comfort in the souls who are willing to listen,
although the number seems to decrease as the years go by.
The more thoughts that swirl about the woman behind the
trees,
the more likely the weeping woman will be free.

Smitten

Be gentle with your smitten heart.
Wrap it in bubble wrap to protect its fragility.
Be wary of those who borrow it,
don't let them use it for selfish needs.

Your heart can only take so many fractures,
until it is broken beyond repair.
This very thing, lovers tend to dare.
Waging a war against the brain.

Your body needs both your heart and mind to survive.
Don't let them battle or you'll meet your demise.
Only because a soul tossed your heart to the sky,
and let it fall when it was incredibly high.

You may fasten your heart together with clothes pins and tape,
but it will falter with time.
Don't rip out your heart for another,
you need it to survive.

Nature Herself

She worships nature herself,
every complex branch and root.
Each tree and specter of dirt,
like the woods spoke to her.

The wave of the river whistles a tune.
Engraving the story of every wanderer.
She gets lost in the woods daily,
and yet never wants to be found.

She drags her hand on every tree,
breathing in the chill breeze.
There are thumps underneath her palms,
as if the trees' hearts are beating.

The branches sway in the wind,
as if the trees are dancing.
She discovers a heart is buried in the soil,
realizing she is nature herself.

Her First Funeral

She had bows in her hair, and a veil over her eyes.
Mourning over the body that met its demise.
An eerily beautiful corpse lying on the grass.
It resembles her yet differently grotesque.

It is the part of her that died.
The slice of her heart she would try to hide.
The corpse is all her excruciating pain,
it is the woman with a dying brain.

She sheds a tear for the part of her
that sickly loved her own depression.
She didn't have a clue what to love.
Now she can leave this part of herself.

She is a woman at her own funeral,
throwing roses on the grass next to herself.
This is her way of dragging herself out of her personal hell.
Leaving her funeral imperfectly well.

A Tree's Healing

My heart blossomed and bled.
The vines have grown through my skin.
The trees have dragged me to them.
To mend my broken bones in dread.

For now, my body will blend with nature.
The process of healing is painful.
Crackles of broken pieces sounding like twigs.
As I focus on still breathing.

The trees' middle is extending,
following my every breath.
Flowers are quietly weeping,
because they fear my untimely death.

Finally, I crawl from the tree's trunk,
covered in mud and vines.
There will be a daisy grown from my heart.
Proving I survived the tortuous healing process...

And I will be just fine.

Babe, You're Healing

Babe, you were addicted to sadness.
Caught up on traumas that caused your madness.
You were stuck under the rain,
when the sun was just a reach away.

Melancholy was the only tune that sang your name.
Happiness was an idea unnamed.
You were dragging yourself with anchors around your ankles,
when an open ocean was just a day away.

Your child-self thought speaking was pain.
Learned to only scream your anguish in your brain.
You taped your mouth shut with tears in your eyes.
Even wished for your own untimely demise.

Darling, at one point you wanted death.
Wished to take your last unwavering breath.
The truth is you never wanted to die,
you just never felt like you were living.

You felt like a ghost in your past.
So, you figured your soul should rejoin your body at last.
But you pulled yourself out of your grave.
For once, you felt like you were brave.

Babe, you are a force to be reckoned with.
You were born with sadness,
but are reborn with beautiful happiness.

You made a fool of your demons,
and killed your death instead.